PASTA

Cooking with Style

Thunder Bay
P·R·E·S·S

Published by
Thunder Bay Press
5880 Oberlin Drive, Suite 400
San Diego, California 92121

Produced by Weldon Russell Pty Ltd
107 Union Street, North Sydney, NSW 2060, Australia

A member of the Weldon International Group of Companies

Copyright © 1994 Weldon Russell Pty Ltd

Publisher: Elaine Russell
Publishing manager: Susan Hurley
Author and home economist: Jane Hann
Editor: Kayte Nunn
US cooking consultant: Mardee Haidin Regan
Designer: Catherine Martin
Photographer: Rowan Fotheringham
Food stylist: Jane Hann
Production: Dianne Leddy

Library of Congress Cataloging-in-Publication data

Hann, Jane, 1955–
    Pasta / [author and home economist, Jane Hann ; photographer, Rowan Fotheringham].
        p.   cm. — (Cooking with style)
    ISBN 1–57145–000–9 : $13.95
        1. Cookery (Pasta)   I. Title.   II. Series.
    TX809.M17H36   1994
    641.8'22—dc20   93-49626
                                                              CIP

Printed by Tien Wah Press, Singapore

A KEVIN WELDON PRODUCTION

Acknowledgments: Waterford Wedgwood; Pillivuyt; Villeroy & Boch; Lillywhites, Sydney; Incorporated Agencies, Sydney; Country Floors, Sydney; HAG Imports, Sydney; Strattons, Sydney

Cover: *Tagliatelle with Prosciutto and Radicchio*
Back cover: *Summer Spaghetti*
Opposite: *Shell Pasta Salad with Shrimp and Red Bell Pepper Mayonnaise* (recipe on page 96)

CONTENTS

Pasta and Seafood Bouillabaisse   50
Linguine with Smoked Salmon and Herb Sauce   52

Vegetables

Tagliatelle in Creamy Sauce with Asparagus   54
Rigatoni with Pumpkin and Bacon Sauce   56
Rigatoni with Roasted Tomato, Red Bell Pepper and Garlic   58
Penne with Mushroom and Tarragon Cream   60
Summer Spaghetti   62

Herbs & Nuts

Farfalle with Onion and Herb Sauce   64
Penne with Chili Chard   66
Gnocchi with Pesto   68
Spaghettini with Coriander and Hazelnut Pesto   70
Fusilli with Pecan and Cream Cheese Sauce   72
Linguine with Almond and Avocado Sauce   74

Baked Pasta

Baked Eggplant, Tomato and Pasta Gratin   76
Individual Rataouille Lasagne   78
Asparagus and Ham Lasagne Rolls   80
Red Bell Peppers Stuffed with Orzo and Tuna   82
Stuffed Pasta Shells in Tomato Sauce   84
Canneloni Stuffed with Ham and Ricotta   86

Desserts

Lemon Pasta Envelopes with Cream Cheese Filling   88
Fresh Figs with Almond Mascarpone and Deep-fried Pasta Wedges   90
Individual Orzo Puddings   92
Date and Ricotta Ravioli Dessert   94

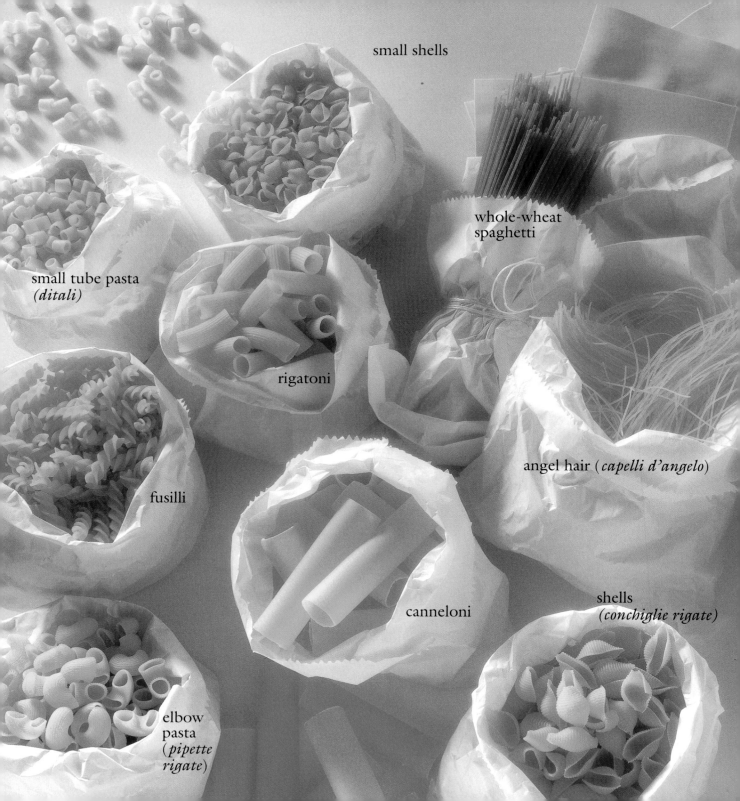

small shells

whole-wheat spaghetti

small tube pasta (*ditali*)

rigatoni

angel hair (*capelli d'angelo*)

fusilli

canneloni

shells (*conchiglie rigate*)

elbow pasta (*pipette rigate*)

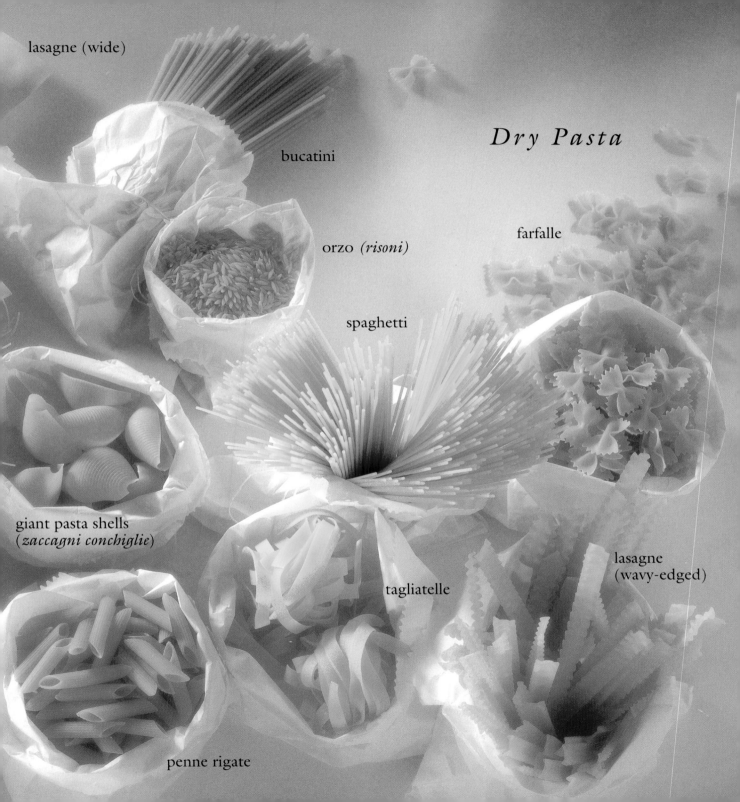

lasagne (wide)

bucatini

Dry Pasta

orzo *(risoni)*

farfalle

spaghetti

giant pasta shells
(*zaccagni conchiglie*)

tagliatelle

lasagne
(wavy-edged)

penne rigate

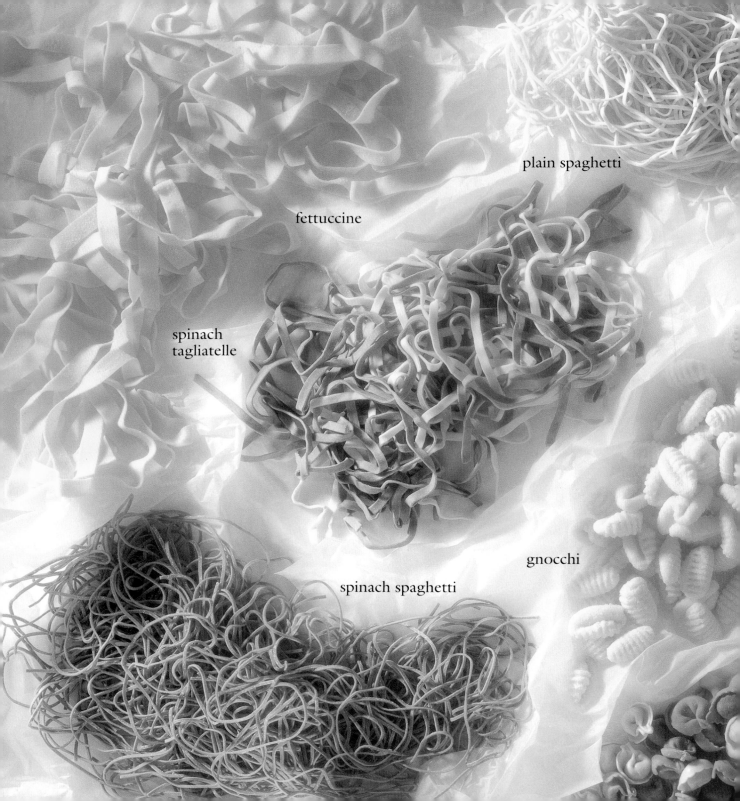

plain spaghetti

fettuccine

spinach
tagliatelle

gnocchi

spinach spaghetti

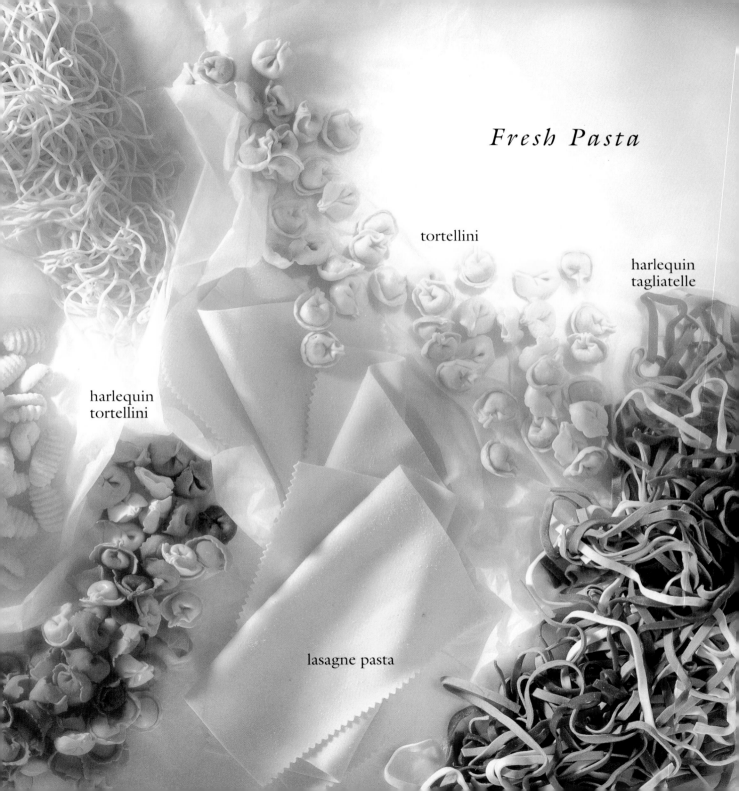

Fresh Pasta

tortellini

harlequin
tagliatelle

harlequin
tortellini

lasagne pasta

Making your own Pasta

1 cup (5 oz/155 g) unsifted all-purpose (plain) flour
1 cup (5 oz/155 g) semolina
3 eggs, lightly beaten
1 tablespoon olive oil
1 good pinch salt
a little water, if necessary

Makes: 1 lb (500 g)

By Hand

3. Knead the dough for 10 minutes until smooth and elastic. Allow the dough to rest, wrapped in plastic, for 1 hour.

1. Place the flour and semolina in a mixing bowl. Mix thoroughly. Make a well in the center and add the eggs and the oil. Work the eggs and oil thoroughly into the flour.

4. Divide the mixture into four parts. Roll out each part of the dough to the desired thickness and length.

2. When all of the egg is mixed with the flour, bring together to form a ball.

5. Roll up the pasta sheet to form a firm roll. Slice the roll to form strips of pasta.

By Machine

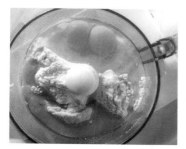

1. Place eggs, oil and flour in the food processor.

2. Process until the mixture forms a ball.

3. Knead the dough until it is smooth and elastic. Divide into four equal quantities. Hand roll into a rectangular shape. Set your pasta machine on its widest setting and roll the pasta several times, folding it in half after each pass.

4. Continue rolling the pasta dough through the machine, adjusting the machine to progressively finer settings with each pass until it is the desired thickness.

5. To cut the pasta into fettuccine or a finer width, roll the dough through the appropriate attachment for the desired width.

Fresh Pasta Variations

Whole-wheat Pasta

Combine 5 oz (155 g) all-purpose (plain) flour with 5 oz (155 g) whole-wheat flour and 3 eggs, beaten. A little water may be necessary to bind it together. Proceed as for plain pasta.

Spinach Pasta

Add ¼ cup (2 oz/60 g) of finely chopped, cooked spinach that has been squeezed to remove all excess moisture, to the eggs and then mix into the flour. Proceed as for plain pasta.

Fresh Herb Pasta

A single herb or mixture of herbs can be used. The herbs must be washed, dried and finely chopped. Add ½ cup (½ oz/15 g) of fresh herbs to flour and proceed as for plain pasta dough.

Tomato Pasta

Add 1 tablespoon of tomato paste or purée to the eggs before adding to the flour and mix well. Proceed as for plain pasta dough.

Useful Information for Cooking Pasta

A few simple guidelines should be followed when preparing pasta:

1. When making fresh pasta, allow the dough to rest for at least 30 minutes in the refrigerator before rolling it out and putting it through the pasta machine.

2. Flour the fresh pasta thoroughly before putting it through the machine. This will prevent it sticking in the machine and is especially important before feeding the pasta through the cutting section of the machine.

3. The choice of ingredients is important. Always choose the best quality pasta, whether it be dried or fresh. The freshest ingredients available should also be used in the sauce; this is particularly important when using herbs. Freshly grated Parmesan cheese is far superior to pre-grated and packaged.

4. Where a recipe calls for the addition of Parmesan, mix it into the freshly cooked pasta before the sauce itself. This will enhance the flavor of the dish far more than sprinkling it over the pasta and sauce.

5. Pasta should never be over-cooked. "*Al dente*" is the term used to describe perfectly cooked pasta — just tender and still a little resistant.

6. A few drops of olive oil added to the boiling water before the pasta will prevent the pasta sticking.

7. A tall, large capacity saucepan is essential for cooking pasta to ensure there is sufficient water. The approximate ratio of dry pasta to boiling water is 3½ oz (100 g) to 32 fl oz (1 liter). Salt the water before adding the pasta, and allow 2 tablespoons of salt to 3½ quarts (3½ liters) of water.

8. The quantity of sauce should be sufficient to coat the pasta thoroughly but not smother it. The pasta should always remain dominant in the dish.

9. Dried pasta needs approximately 10 minutes cooking time — start testing it after 8 minutes. Freshly made pasta, however, is much faster. It should be ready within approximately 3 minutes, but start testing it after 2 minutes.

Lasagne with Broccoli and Mustard Sauce

7 tablespoons (3½ oz/100 g)
  butter, softened

1 tablespoon strong Dijon
  mustard

3 scallions (shallots), finely diced

2 cloves garlic, crushed

2 tablespoons roughly chopped
  flat-leaf parsley

2 teaspoons fresh tarragon leaves

1 lb (500 g) broccoli, broken into
  small pieces

8 oz (250 g) lasagne pasta

¾ cup (6 fl oz/185 ml) crème
  fraîche or light sour cream

2 tablespoons sliced sun-dried
  tomatoes

grated zest of 1 lemon

salt and freshly ground black
  pepper

1½ oz (45 g) slivered (flaked)
  almonds, toasted

In a food processor, combine the butter, mustard, scallions (shallots), garlic, parsley and tarragon. Process until well combined.

Bring a large saucepan of water to a boil. Blanch the broccoli and retain the water for the pasta. Put the pasta on to cook.

Melt the mustard butter over low heat and allow to bubble for 1–2 minutes. Stir in the crème fraîche, followed by the sun-dried tomatoes and the lemon zest. Warm sauce thoroughly but do not allow to boil. Add the broccoli to the sauce and heat through. Season with salt and freshly ground black pepper.

Drain the pasta and put onto a warmed serving plate. Pour broccoli and sauce over the pasta. Sprinkle with toasted almonds and serve immediately.

Serves 6 as a side dish or an appetizer
Preparation/Cooking Time: 30 minutes

Filled Pasta Shell Salad

8 oz (250 g) jumbo-size pasta
  shells
2 tablespoons finely chopped
  coriander (cilantro)
1 tablespoon finely chopped chervil

Dressing:
2 small fresh chili peppers, finely
  chopped
1 clove garlic, crushed
2 tablespoons olive oil
1 tablespoon balsamic vinegar
juice of 4 limes

Filling:
13 oz (410 g) butternut squash
  (pumpkin)
1 large Spanish (purple) onion,
  diced
½ large red bell pepper
  (capsicum), diced

Dressing: Combine all the dressing ingredients and whisk together until well blended.

Filling: Cut the squash (pumpkin) into slices and steam gently until just tender. Set aside to cool. When cool, cut the squash into small slices.

In a bowl, combine the squash, onion, bell pepper (capsicum) and two-thirds of the prepared dressing. Mix well, then set aside.

Cook the pasta in boiling water until tender. Drain and run under cold water; set aside to cool.

When the pasta is cool, carefully spoon the squash mixture into the shells and arrange them on a serving dish; drizzle the remaining dressing over the shells.

Garnish with the coriander (cilantro) and chervil.

Serves 4
Preparation/Cooking Time: 30 minutes

Pasta Salad Niçoise

Dressing:
2 tablespoons red wine vinegar
1 tablespoon lemon juice
1 teaspoon Dijon mustard
½ teaspoon sugar
1 clove garlic, crushed
Salt and black pepper
½ cup (4 fl oz/125 ml) olive oil

¼ cup (2 fl oz/60 ml) olive oil
1 clove garlic, crushed
10 oz (315 g) fresh tuna, skinned and sliced
8 oz (250 g) shell pasta
8 oz (250 g) green beans trimmed, cut into 2-in (5-cm) lengths and blanched
10 oz (315 g) cherry tomatoes
6½ oz (200 g) yellow teardrop tomatoes (optional)
3½ oz (100 g) small, black olives
1 jar (6 oz/185 g) marinated artichoke hearts, halved
4 hard-cooked eggs, peeled and quartered
1 tablespoon each chopped parsley, basil and chives
1 can (2 oz/60 g) anchovy fillets, drained

Dressing: Combine all ingredients in a jar and shake well. Cook the pasta in boiling salted water until *al dente*. Run under cold water, drain thoroughly and allow to cool.

Heat the oil in a frying pan and sauté the garlic for about 30 seconds. Add the tuna and cook gently for a minute or two on both sides until it is just cooked, but still rare in the middle. (Canned tuna can be used if fresh is unavailable.) Remove from the pan, drain on a paper towel and allow to cool.

To make the salad, combine all of the remaining ingredients with the tuna. Pour over the desired quantity of dressing. Stir carefully and thoroughly to coat all ingredients with the dressing.

Serves 4–6
Preparation/Cooking Time: 45 minutes

Shell Pasta with Goat Cheese and Basil Vinaigrette

Basil Vinaigrette:

1 cup (1 oz/30 g) loosely packed
   fresh basil leaves
2 small cloves garlic, chopped
1 tablespoon red wine vinegar
salt and freshly ground black
   pepper
¼ cup (2 fl oz/60 ml) plus 2
   tablespoons olive oil, extra

8 oz (250 g) small shell pasta
6½ oz (200 g) goat cheese,
   crumbled
6½ oz (200 g) cherry tomatoes,
   halved
3½ oz (100 g) small black olives
4 wedges of focaccia
3 tablespoons toasted pine nuts

Basil Vinaigrette: Place the basil, garlic, vinegar and salt and pepper in food processor. Process until the basil is finely chopped. Add the ¼ cup of oil and process again until emulsified.

Cook the pasta in boiling salted water until *al dente*. Run under cold water and drain thoroughly. Toss through enough of the basil vinaigrette to coat shells thoroughly. Add the goat cheese and mix thoroughly. Add the tomatoes and olives and stir to combine. Add some more dressing, if necessary, but do not make the mixture too wet.

Toast the focaccia wedges and brush with a little of the extra oil. Serve the wedges piled with the pasta mixture and sprinkled with toasted pine nuts.

Serves 4 as appetizer or luncheon dish
Preparation/Cooking Time: 30 minutes

Fresh Herb Pasta

1 lb fresh pasta, made according to instructions given on page 12, preferably using a pasta machine

½ cup (½–¾ oz/10–20 g) each, dill, fresh coriander (cilantro), flat-leaf parsley leaves, washed and carefully dried

⅓ cup (2½ fl oz/75 ml) olive oil

3 cloves garlic, finely chopped

2 tablespoons finely chopped flat-leaf parsley

freshly ground black pepper

Parmesan cheese shavings

Divide the dough into 3 pieces. Cover 2 pieces with plastic wrap to prevent them from drying out. On a lightly floured surface, or using a pasta machine, roll out 1 piece into a very thin sheet. Distribute one-third of the herb leaves over half of the sheet. Carefully flatten each leaf in place. Lightly brush the uncovered half of the sheet with water and fold it over the side with the leaves. Press down firmly to seal the leaves in and force out any air bubbles.

Roll the folded sheet through the pasta machine once to make a very thin sheet of pasta. With a sharp knife or pasta cutter cut the sheet into 2-inch (5-cm) squares. Repeat the procedure with the remaining dough and leaves.

Cook the pasta in boiling salted water until *al dente*, about 2 minutes.

Heat the oil in a frying pan. Add the garlic and cook gently for 1 minute. Add the parsley and pepper.

Drain the pasta. Toss through the oil and garlic. Garnish with Parmesan shavings, if desired. Serve immediately.

Serves 4–6. This dish makes a good accompaniment for veal or served as an appetizer on its own.
Preparation/Cooking Time: 1 hour

Skewered Tricolor Tortellini

1 lb (500 g) mixed tortellini
  (green, yellow, red)

Dressing:
¼ cup (2 fl oz/60 ml) plus 3
  tablespoons extra-virgin olive oil
1 tablespoon balsamic vinegar
salt and freshly ground black
  pepper

1 endive (baby chicory), washed
  and torn
1 small radicchio, washed and
  torn
1 bunch arugula (rocket), washed
  and torn
½ bunch watercress, washed and
  stemmed
2 tablespoons (1 oz/30 g) butter
1 clove garlic, crushed
½ cup (4 fl oz/125 ml) light
  (single) cream
1¾ oz (50 g) freshly grated
  Parmesan cheese
1 tablespoon chopped fresh parsley
1 tablespoon chopped fresh basil
Parmesan cheese shavings, for
  serving

B ring a large saucepan of salted water to a boil. Add the tortellini and cook until the tortellini is tender. Drain.

Dressing: Combine all the dressing ingredients in a jar and shake vigorously.

Arrange the salad greens on individual serving plates. Drizzle with some dressing.

Heat the butter in a small saucepan. Stir in the garlic and cook for 1 minute. Stir in the cream, Parmesan, parsley and basil. Cook for 1 minute. Add the drained tortellini to the pan and stir to coat the tortellini thoroughly. Set aside for 5 minutes to cool slightly.

Thread the tortellini onto wooden skewers. Serve on individual salad plates, allowing 2–3 skewers per person. Scatter with Parmesan shavings.

Serves 4–6
Preparation/Cooking Time: 30 minutes

Warm Whole-wheat Spaghetti with Red Cabbage and Goat Cheese

1 tablespoon walnut oil

2 tablespoons olive oil

1 cup (3½ oz/100g) shelled walnuts, roughly chopped

8 oz (250 g) whole-wheat spaghetti

1 clove garlic, chopped

2 tablespoons balsamic vinegar

1 red onion, thinly sliced

½ small red cabbage, finely shredded

salt and freshly ground black pepper

1 large green apple, cut into julienne

1 tablespoon finely chopped parsley

3½ oz (100 g) goat cheese, crumbled

Heat the walnut and olive oils together and sauté the walnuts, stirring constantly, for 2 minutes. Remove from heat. Put the walnuts on a paper towel to drain. Reserve the oil in a frying pan.

Bring a saucepan of salted water to a boil and put the pasta on to cook.

Add the garlic and vinegar to the remaining oil in the pan. As soon as the mixture is hot, add the onion and sauté for 30 seconds. Add the cabbage and stir-fry for 1–2 minutes, until the cabbage is just wilted. Season with salt and pepper. Add the apple and parsley and cook for another 30 seconds. Stir in half the walnuts.

Drain the pasta and stir in the goat cheese while the pasta is still hot. Toss the cabbage mixture carefully through the pasta and serve warm, garnished with the remaining walnuts.

Serves 6 as an appetizer or accompaniment
Preparation/Cooking Time: 30 minutes

Individual Tortellini Salad

1 lb (500 g) store-bought tortellini
filled with ham and ricotta
6½ oz (200 g) cherry tomatoes
3½ oz (100 g) tiny black olives
1 bunch arugula (rocket), washed
and dried
1 cup (1 oz/30 g) shredded basil
leaves
6½ oz (200 g) spicy salami, cut
into thin strips
2 small red onions, cut into thin
rings
10 sun-dried tomatoes, cut into
strips
½ cup (1¾ oz/50 g) Parmesan
shavings

Dressing:
½ cup (4 fl oz/125 ml)
extra-virgin olive oil
2 tablespoons balsamic vinegar
1 small clove garlic, crushed
Salt and freshly ground black
pepper

Bring a large saucepan of salted water to a boil. Add the tortellini and cook until tender.

Dressing: Combine all the dressing ingredients in a jar and shake vigorously.

Drain the tortellini thoroughly and place in a shallow baking dish. Pour on two-thirds of the dressing and gently toss to coat each piece thoroughly. Allow the tortellini to cool to room temperature.

When the pasta has cooled make salads on individual plates, arranging all the ingredients decoratively. Top with Parmesan shavings.

Just before serving, drizzle on a little more dressing.

Serves 4
Preparation/Cooking Time: 30 minutes

Bucatini with Ginger Carrots

1 lb (500 g) carrots, cut into
  julienne
7 tablespoons (3½ oz/100 g)
  butter
2 teaspoons brown sugar
2 teaspoons white wine vinegar
1 tablespoon cumin seeds
1 piece (⅓ in/1 cm) fresh ginger,
  finely chopped
4 tablespoons coconut milk
3 tablespoons finely chopped fresh
  coriander (cilantro)
8 oz (250 g) bucatini (hollow,
  spaghetti-shaped pasta)
toasted sesame seeds, for garnish

Steam the carrots until just tender. Melt the butter in a frying pan and stir in the sugar and vinegar until the mixture is well combined. Add the cumin seeds and ginger and cook for a few minutes. Add the coconut milk and warm gently. Add the cooked carrots and coriander (cilantro) and warm through.

Cook the pasta in boiling salted water until *al dente*. Drain and stir into the carrot mixture. Serve immediately in warmed bowls. Garnish with toasted sesame seeds.

Serves 4 as an appetizer
Preparation/Cooking Time: 30 minutes

Pasta, Lentil and Pepperoni Soup

1 cup (6½ oz/200 g) red lentils
4 cups (32 fl oz/1 l) chicken stock
1 bay leaf
1 tablespoon olive oil
1 large onion, finely chopped
1 (14 oz/440 g) can tomatoes,
  undrained and tomatoes
  roughly chopped
8 oz (250 g) small tube pasta or
  similar short pasta
6½ oz (200 g) pepperoni, thinly
  sliced

Place the lentils, chicken stock and bay leaf in a large saucepan. Bring to a boil, reduce heat and simmer for 1–1¼ hours, until the lentils are very soft. Purée the mixture in a food processor and return to the saucepan.

Heat the oil in a frying pan and sauté the onion until soft. Add the onion and tomatoes to the soup and simmer gently for 15 minutes.

Cook the pasta in boiling salted water until *al dente*. Drain and stir into the soup, together with the pepperoni.

When all of the ingredients are well heated, serve immediately in warm soup bowls.

Serves 6
Preparation/Cooking Time: 1 hour 30 minutes

Tagliatelle and Chick-Pea Soup

8 oz (250 g) dried chick-peas
(garbanzo beans), soaked
overnight in cold water and
drained
5 oz (155 g) tagliatelle
3 tablespoons olive oil
1 large onion, finely chopped
2 cloves garlic, finely chopped
1 large sprig fresh rosemary
2 teaspoons tomato paste

Place the chick-peas (garbanzo beans) in lightly salted water in a saucepan. Bring to a boil, reduce heat and simmer until tender, about 1 hour.

Place two-thirds of the chick-peas in a food processor with their cooking water. Process until smooth.

Cook the pasta in boiling salted water until *al dente*.

Heat the oil in a frying pan. Add the onion, garlic and rosemary and sauté gently. Add the tomato paste and stir thoroughly. Add the puréed chick peas, whole chick-peas, the onion mixture and pasta. Heat through thoroughly.

Remove the rosemary sprig and serve immediately in warmed soup bowls.

Serves 4
Preparation/Cooking Time: 1 hour

Macaroni and Bean Soup

1 cup (6½ oz/200 g) dried white
    beans, soaked overnight in cold
    water and drained
4 oz (125 g) macaroni pasta
14 oz (440 g) speck, pancetta or
    smoked bacon, cubed
2 large onions, chopped
1 clove garlic, finely chopped
4 large tomatoes, chopped
7 cups (56 fl oz/1.75 l) vegetable
    stock
1 bouquet garni — 1 large sprig
    thyme, oregano and parsley tied
    together and wrapped in
    cheesecloth
salt and freshly ground black
    pepper
2 tablespoons chopped parsley, for
    garnish (optional)

Combine all the ingredients in a large saucepan. Bring to a boil, reduce the heat and simmer for 1–1½ hours, or until the beans are cooked through. Season to taste with salt and pepper.

Serve in warm soup bowls and sprinkle with the chopped parsley, if desired.

Serves 6
Preparation/Cooking Time: 2 hours

Thai-style Chicken and Pasta Soup

1 tablespoon vegetable oil

1 red bell pepper (capsicum), seeds
  and membrane removed and
  cut into thin strips

4 green (spring) onions, sliced

1 clove garlic, crushed

4 boneless, skinless chicken thighs
  or breasts, cut into thin strips

6½ oz (200 g) button mushrooms

3 cups (24 fl oz/750 ml)
  good-quality chicken stock

1 cup (8 fl oz/250 ml) water

¾ cup plus 2 tablespoons (7 fl oz/
  220 ml) unsweetened coconut
  milk

2 medium tomatoes, peeled, seeded
  and finely chopped

¼ cup (¼ oz/7 g) chopped fresh
  coriander (cilantro)

1 cup (3½ oz/100 g) bean sprouts

1–2 heaped teaspoons curry paste

4 oz (125 g) angel hair (capelli
  d'angelo) pasta

Garnishes:

2 tablespoons toasted thread
  coconut, chopped fresh coriander
  (cilantro), sliced green (spring)
  onions

In a large saucepan, heat the oil and cook the bell pepper (capsicum), green (spring) onions and garlic for 2–3 minutes. Add the chicken and cook 2 minutes longer, or until the chicken changes color. Slice the mushrooms and add to the pan. Cook for 2 minutes.

Stir in all of the remaining ingredients except the pasta and bring to a boil. Add the pasta, reduce the heat, and simmer for 10–15 minutes, or until the pasta is cooked and the chicken is tender. Add a little more water if the soup becomes too thick. Serve in warm soup bowls, garnished with coconut, green (spring) onions and coriander (cilantro).

Serves 4–6
Preparation/Cooking Time: 45 minutes

Fettuccine with Chicken, Avocado and Creamy Rosemary Sauce

3 tablespoons butter

2 large onions, finely diced

¼ cup (2 fl oz/60 ml) brandy

¼ cup (1 oz/30 g) all-purpose (plain) flour

1 teaspoon salt

1 teaspoon paprika

1 tablespoon fresh rosemary (or 1½ teaspoons dried)

freshly ground black pepper

2 cups (16 fl oz/500 ml) chicken stock

1¼ cups (10 fl oz/315 ml) sour cream

½ cup (4 fl oz/125 ml) milk

1½ lb (750 g) cooked chicken, cut into bite-size pieces

1 lb (500 g) fettuccine (mixture of spinach, tomato and egg fettuccine)

1 large avocado, peeled, pitted and diced

In a large saucepan melt the butter and add the onions. Sauté gently until the onions are well cooked and starting to brown. Add the brandy and simmer until almost all the liquid is absorbed. Gradually stir in the flour and cook until thickened. Add the salt, paprika, rosemary and pepper, and stir. Gently cook for about 2 minutes. Gradually add the chicken stock and bring the mixture to a boil. Boil gently for 3 minutes.

Remove saucepan from heat and gradually beat in the sour cream and then the milk. Finally add the chicken. Return the saucepan to low heat and simmer gently for 15 minutes.

While the sauce is cooking, bring a large saucepan of water to a boil and cook the pasta until *al dente*.

Just prior to serving, add the diced avocado to the sauce and fold through.

Drain the pasta and divide among the serving bowls. Spoon on the chicken sauce and serve immediately.

Serves 6
Preparation/Cooking Time: 45 minutes

Tagliatelle with Prosciutto and Radicchio

1 lb (500 g) tagliatelle
salt
6½ oz (200 g) prosciutto
7 tablespoons (3½ oz/100 g)
  butter
2 tablspoons olive oil
⅓ cup (⅓ oz/10 g) finely shredded
  basil
8 leaves radicchio, washed and
  finely shredded
⅓ cup plus 2 tablespoons (3½ oz/
  100 g) freshly grated Parmesan
  cheese, plus extra shavings, for
  garnish
freshly ground black pepper

Cook the pasta in boiling salted water until *al dente*. Drain well and return the pasta to the pan with the butter.

Fry the prosciutto in the olive oil until crisp. Drain on paper towels and then crumble.

In a bowl, combine the basil, radicchio, Parmesan, pepper and half of the prosciutto.

Finally, add the pasta to the bowl and toss quickly and thoroughly through the sauce. Distribute among warmed pasta bowls, top with Parmesan shavings and the remaining prosciutto.

Serves 4–6
Preparation/Cooking Time: 40 minutes

Fettuccine with Salmon and Mushrooms

1 tablespoon butter

3 green (spring) onions, finely
    chopped

8 oz (250 g) button mushrooms,
    wiped clean and sliced

1 cup (8 fl oz/250 ml) heavy
    (whipping) cream

1 tablespoon tomato paste

6½ oz (200 g) canned red salmon,
    any skin and bone removed,
    meat broken into small pieces

1 lb (500 g) fettuccine

Melt the butter and gently sauté the green (spring) onions until almost cooked. Add the mushrooms and cook for 2–3 minutes. Add the cream and tomato paste and stir over low heat until the tomato paste is completely mixed into the sauce. Add the salmon and simmer gently for 1–2 minutes.

Cook the pasta in boiling salted water until *al dente*. Drain and stir into sauce. Serve immediately in warmed bowls.

Note: This sauce can be made 1–2 hours ahead and reheated gently when required.

Serves 4
Preparation/Cooking Time: 20 minutes

Farfalle with Bacon and Leek Cream Sauce

8 oz (250 g) bacon
4 tablespoons (1¾ oz/50 g) butter
2 cloves garlic, finely chopped
1½ lb (750 g) baby leeks, well-
    washed, trimmed, and
    finely sliced
1 cup (8 fl oz/250 ml) light
    (single) cream
½ cup (4 fl oz/125 ml) dry white
    wine
⅓ cup (2½ fl oz/75 ml) sour
    cream
¾ cup plus 2 tablespoons (3½ oz/
    100 g) Parmesan cheese, freshly
    grated
freshly ground black pepper
¾ cup (3½ oz/100 g) walnuts,
    roughly chopped
1 lb (500 g) farfalle (bow-tie
    pasta)

Remove any excess fat from the bacon and cut it into large dice. Sauté in a small frying pan until crisp. Drain on absorbent paper and set aside.

Heat 3½ tablespoons of the butter in a large frying pan and add the garlic and leeks. Cook gently over low heat until leeks are very soft. Add the cream, sour cream, wine and Parmesan cheese and stir until the mixture is well heated and slightly thickened. Do not allow to boil. Stir in the bacon. Add pepper to taste.

Melt the remaining butter in a small pan. Add the walnuts and toss until lightly toasted.

Cook the farfalle pasta until *al dente*. Drain well. Add the sauce to coat pasta thoroughly. Serve in individual warmed pasta bowls, garnished with the walnuts.

Serves 4–6
Preparation/Cooking Time: 30 minutes

Pasta and Seafood Bouillabaisse

2 tablespoons olive oil
1 large onion, chopped
2 cloves garlic, finely chopped
1 small red chili pepper, finely
   chopped
2 cups (16 fl oz/500 ml) fish stock
1 (28 oz/880 g) can plum
   tomatoes, undrained
1 cup (8 fl oz/250 ml) dry white
   wine
4 oz (125g) shell pasta or similar
   short pasta
2 tablespoons chopped fresh basil
salt and freshly ground black
   pepper
16 mussels, beards removed and
   scrubbed
1 lb (500 g) firm white boneless
   fish fillets, cut into 1-in
   (2.5-cm) cubes
8 jumbo shrimp (prawns), shelled
   and deveined with tails intact

In a large saucepan heat the oil and the cook the onion, garlic and chili for 4–5 minutes, until the onion is soft. Add the stock, tomatoes and wine. Bring to a boil and simmer for 25–30 minutes.

While the sauce is cooking, cook the pasta in boiling salted water until *al dente*.

Stir the basil, salt and pepper into the tomato sauce. Add the mussels, cover and cook for 2–3 minutes. Add the fish and shrimp (prawns) and simmer over low heat for 2–3 minutes until they are just cooked. Discard any mussels that have not opened. Stir in cooked pasta and allow to heat through.

Serve immediately in warm bowls with crusty bread.

Serves 4
Preparation/Cooking Time: 45 minutes

Linguine with Smoked Salmon and Herb Sauce

6½ oz (200 g) smoked salmon
1 cup (8 fl oz/200 ml) heavy
  (whipping) cream
1 tablespoon chopped chives
1 tablespoon chopped dill
1 lb (500 g) fresh linguine
whipped cream, salmon caviar,
  chives and dill, to garnish

Roughly chop half of the smoked salmon and combine in a food processor with the cream. Process just long enough to make the mixture smooth; avoid whipping the cream. Pour the cream mixture into a saucepan, add the chopped chives and dill and warm gently. Cut the remaining salmon into thin strips.

Cook the pasta in boiling salted water until *al dente*. Drain and put into a warm serving bowl. Add the cream sauce and remaining salmon and toss through. Garnish with cream, salmon caviar and herbs.

Serves 4–6
Preparation/Cooking Time: 20 minutes

Tagliatelle in Creamy Sauce with Asparagus

8 oz (250 g) plain tagliatelle
  (fresh or dried)

8 oz (250 g) spinach tagliatelle
  (fresh or dried)

2 tablespoons olive oil

2 medium onions, chopped

2 cloves garlic, crushed

6 scallions (shallots), chopped

½ cup (4 fl oz/125 ml) dry white
  wine

1¼ cups (10 fl oz/315 ml) heavy
  (whipping) cream

⅓ cup (3 fl oz/90 ml) sour cream

⅓ cup (⅓ oz/10 g) shredded fresh
  basil

1 cup (4 oz/125 g) freshly grated
  Parmesan cheese

1 large bunch asparagus, cut into
  short lengths

extra Parmesan shavings, for
  serving

Cook the pasta in a large pot of boiling salted water. (If using fresh pasta, make the sauce first, as fresh pasta requires only a brief cooking time.) Drain well.

While the pasta is cooking, make the sauce. Heat the oil in a pan, add the onions and garlic and cook until the onions are soft. Add the scallions (shallots) and stir until soft. Stir in the wine, cream, sour cream, basil and grated Parmesan. Stir until heated through — do not boil. Stir the sauce into the pasta.

Just before serving, blanch the asparagus in boiling water until just tender. Drain.

Serve the pasta in warmed bowls; top with the asparagus and Parmesan shavings.

Serves 4–6
Preparation/Cooking Time: 25 minutes

Rigatoni with Pumpkin and Bacon Sauce

3 cups (10 oz/315 g) chopped
  pumpkin flesh or 1¼ cups
  canned pumpkin purée
1 lb (500g) rigatoni
6½ oz (200 g) bacon, cut into dice
1 clove garlic, finely chopped
½ cup (4 fl oz/125 ml) heavy
  (whipping) cream
1 tablespoon finely chopped parsley
freshly ground pepper
1 cup (3½ oz/100 g) freshly
  grated Parmesan cheese

Cut the pumpkin into bite-size pieces and steam until soft. Mash the pumpkin gently.

Cook the pasta in boiling salted water until *al dente*. Drain.

While pasta is cooking, prepare the sauce. Sauté the bacon with the garlic until the bacon is crisp.

Put the mashed pumpkin into a saucepan and gradually stir in the cream. Add the bacon and garlic mixture and the parsley and gently warm the sauce. Season with the pepper.

Stir the grated Parmesan into the drained pasta. Add the sauce and toss to mix well. Serve immediately in heated bowls.

Serves 4–6
Preparation/Cooking Time: 30 minutes

Rigatoni with Roasted Tomato, Red Bell Pepper and Garlic

4 ripe tomatoes
1 large red bell pepper (capsicum), quartered, seeds and membrane removed
1 small head (bulb) garlic, excess papery skin removed
1 tablespoon olive oil
1 tablespoon balsamic vinegar
salt, freshly ground black pepper
1 lb (500 g) rigatoni
3½ oz (100 g) sun-dried tomatoes
3½ oz (100 g) small black olives

Preheat oven to 350°F (180°C/Gas 4). Place the tomatoes, bell pepper (capsicum) and garlic in a baking pan, brush with the oil and bake for 30 minutes.

Remove from the oven and set aside to cool slightly. Squeeze the garlic out of its shells, peel the tomatoes and red pepper and place all in a food processor with the vinegar. Process until the mixture is almost smooth but still has some texture. Season with salt and freshly ground pepper.

Cook the pasta in boiling salted water until *al dente*.

Heat the sauce in a saucepan. Add the sun-dried tomatoes and black olives and warm through thoroughly. Drain the pasta. Stir into the sauce and serve immediately in warmed pasta bowls.

Serves 4–6
Preparation/Cooking Time: 45 minutes

Penne with Mushroom and Tarragon Cream

3½ tablespoons (1¾ oz/50 g)
   butter
8 oz (250 g) small white (button)
   mushrooms
1 clove garlic, crushed
2 teaspoons fresh tarragon, finely
   chopped   1/2 Tsp DRied
salt and freshly ground black
   pepper
1¼ cups (10 fl oz/315 ml) heavy
   (whipping) cream
1 teaspoon grated lemon zest
½ cup (1¾ oz/50 g) freshly grated
   Parmesan cheese
1 lb (500 g) penne

Melt the butter in a frying pan. Add the mushrooms and sauté gently for about 1 minute. Add the garlic and cook for 30 seconds. Add the tarragon, salt and pepper, cream and lemon zest. Stir over low heat for 2 minutes. Add the Parmesan cheese and cook gently for 3 minutes, until the mixture thickens slightly.

Cook the pasta in boiling salted water until *al dente*. Drain and stir into the sauce. Serve immediately.

Serves 4
Preparation/Cooking Time: 20 minutes

Summer Spaghetti

1 lb (500 g) firm ripe tomatoes,
  peeled, seeded and finely
  chopped
1 red onion, diced
1 small red chili pepper, seeds
  removed and very finely chopped
12 stuffed green olives, finely
  chopped
1 tablespoon capers, chopped if
  large
1½ teaspoons finely chopped fresh
  oregano
⅓ cup (⅓ oz/10 g) finely chopped
  parsley
2 cloves garlic, crushed
½ cup (4 fl oz/125 ml)
  extra-virgin olive oil
1 lb (500 g) spaghetti

Combine all of the ingredients except the pasta in a bowl. Mix well; cover and let stand overnight.

Cook pasta in boiling salted water until *al dente*. Serve pasta sauce at room temperature over hot pasta.

Serves 4–6
Preparation/Cooking Time: 30 minutes

Farfalle with Onion and Herb Sauce

1½ tablespoons olive oil
1½ lb (750 g) white onions, thinly
  sliced
1 teaspoon honey
1 pinch nutmeg
2 cloves garlic, crushed
3 cups (750 ml/24 fl oz) chicken
  (or vegetable) stock
1 lb (500 g) farfalle (bow-tie
  pasta)
2 tablespoons freshly grated
  Parmesan cheese
2 teaspoons freshly chopped
  marjoram
1 teaspoon freshly chopped thyme
1½ tablespoons freshly chopped
  parsley
1½ tablespoons sherry vinegar

Heat the oil in a saucepan and cook the onions over medium heat, tossing until well coated. Reduce the heat, cover and sweat onions, stirring occasionally, for 20 minutes. Stir in the honey, nutmeg and garlic and cook for 5 minutes, stirring often. Add the stock and simmer for about 15 minutes, or until the liquid is reduced by half.

While reducing the onion sauce, cook the pasta in boiling salted water until *al dente*. Add the Parmesan, herbs and vinegar to the onion mixture, and then add the pasta. Stir thoroughly and allow the pasta to heat through. Serve immediately in warmed bowls.

Serves 4–6
Preparation/Cooking Time: 1 hour

Penne with Chili Chard

1 lb (500 g) penne
¼ cup (2 fl oz/60 ml) olive oil
1 clove garlic, finely chopped
1 red onion, finely chopped
1 small red chili pepper, seeded
  and finely chopped
3½ oz (100 g) coppacolla or
  smoked bacon, diced
8 stalks Swiss chard, or spinach,
  washed, hard stalk removed and
  shredded
salt and freshly ground black
  pepper
½ cup (2 oz/60 g) freshly grated
  Parmesan cheese

Cook the pasta in boiling salted water while preparing the chard mixture.

Heat the oil in a frying pan and add the garlic, onion, chili and coppacolla. Cook for 2 minutes. Add the chard and stir-fry until the chard just starts to wilt. Season to taste with salt and pepper.

Drain the pasta, return it to the saucepan and stir in the Parmesan. Add the chard mixture, stir thoroughly. Serve immediately.

Serves 4
Preparation/Cooking Time: 25 minutes

Gnocchi with Pesto

1 large bunch fresh basil, washed
  and leaves removed from stems
1–2 cloves garlic, roughly chopped
1 cup (3½ oz/100 g) freshly grated
  Parmesan cheese
2 tablespoons pine nuts
1 teaspoon salt
½ cup (4 fl oz/125 ml)
  extra-virgin olive oil
1 lb (500 g) store-bought fresh
  gnocchi
grated Parmesan cheese, for
  serving
2 tablespoons toasted pine nuts
  (optional), for serving

Place the basil, garlic, Parmesan, pine nuts and salt in a food processor. Process until the ingredients are chopped. While the motor is running, drizzle in the olive oil, until the ingredients are finely chopped and the mixture is smooth.

Bring some water to a boil in a large saucepan. Add some salt and the gnocchi to the boiling water. The gnocchi is cooked when it comes to the surface of the water. As soon as the gnocchi is cooked, drain it and place in a warmed serving bowl. Pour on the pesto and mix carefully but thoroughly. Serve immediately with extra grated cheese and toasted pine nuts, if desired.

Serves 4–6
Preparation/Cooking Time: 15 minutes

Spaghettini with Coriander and Hazelnut Pesto

1 lb (500 g) spaghettini
1 cup (3½ oz/100 g) hazelnuts, toasted in the oven, skins removed and roughly chopped
1 bunch (1¾ oz/50 g) fresh coriander (cilantro) leaves, washed and dried
1 small clove garlic, chopped
1 teaspoon salt
2 tablespoons hazelnut oil or olive oil
3 tablespoons olive oil
1 tablespoon butter
1 cup (3½ oz/100 g) freshly grated Parmesan cheese

Cook the pasta in boiling salted water until *al dente*. While the pasta is cooking, prepare the pesto. Place the hazelnuts, coriander (cilantro), garlic and salt in a food processor. Process until the ingredients are roughly chopped. While the motor is running, gradually pour in the hazelnut oil and olive oil. The mixture should be well chopped and mixed but not puréed.

Drain the pasta and put into a warmed serving bowl. Stir in the butter and Parmesan. Quickly add the pesto, and mix until the pasta is thoroughly coated.

Serve immediately in warmed pasta bowls. Extra Parmesan can be sprinkled over individual servings, if desired.

Serves 4–6
Cooking/Preparation Time: 20 minutes

Fusilli with Pecan and Cream Cheese Sauce

3 tablespoons (1½ oz/45 g) butter
1 clove garlic, finely chopped
5 oz (155 g) pecans, chopped
1 lb (500 g) fusilli
5 oz (155 g) cream cheese
½ cup (4 fl oz/125 ml) heavy
    (whipping) cream
½ cup (1¾ oz/50 g) freshly grated
    Parmesan cheese

In a large frying pan, melt the butter and gently fry the garlic until golden. Add the pecans and sauté for 3 minutes. Remove from heat.

Cook the pasta in boiling salted water until *al dente*.

Add the cream cheese to the pecans and heat gently. Gradually stir in the cream and continue cooking gently until the mixture is warmed through.

Drain the pasta. Stir in the Parmesan and toss. Add the sauce, toss through and serve at once in warmed pasta bowls.

Serves 6
Preparation/Cooking Time: 30 minutes

Linguine with Almond and Avocado Sauce

½ cup (4 fl oz/125 ml) plus 2
   tablespoons olive oil
2 medium onions, diced
2 cloves garlic, chopped
salt
½ cup (½ oz/15 g) shredded basil
   leaves
1 cup (3½ oz/100 g) unblanched
   almonds, roughly chopped
flesh of 2 medium avocados,
   mashed
freshly ground black pepper
juice of 1 large lemon
1 lb (500 g) linguine

In a frying pan, heat 2 tablespoons of the olive oil and sauté the onions until translucent. Add the garlic and salt to taste, cover the frying pan and cook gently until soft.

In a food processor, combine the onion mixture, basil, almonds, avocados and pepper. While the motor is running, slowly drizzle in the remaining ½ cup olive oil and the lemon juice. Process until the mixture reaches the desired consistency.

Cook the pasta in boiling salted water until *al dente*. Warm the sauce just prior to using and stir into the hot pasta.

Garnish with a few roughly chopped, unblanched almonds.

Serves 4–6
Preparation/Cooking Time: 30 minutes

Baked Eggplant, Tomato and Pasta Gratin

3 medium eggplants (aubergines)
  (about 3 lb/1.5 kg)
2 tablespoons olive oil
2 onions, chopped
2 cloves garlic, chopped
1 can (14 oz/440 g) plum
  tomatoes, undrained
2 tablespoons tomato paste
2 teaspoons dried basil
1 teaspoon dried oregano
salt and freshly ground black
  pepper
2–3 tablespoons extra olive oil, for
  frying eggplant
8 oz (250 g) penne or other short
  pasta
10 oz (315 g) mozzarella cheese,
  sliced

Wash the eggplants (aubergines) and cut crosswise into thin slices. Arrange the slices in a colander and sprinkle the cut surfaces with salt. Let stand for about 30 minutes to allow the bitter juices to degorge. Rinse the eggplant slices under cold running water. Arrange the slices on paper towels and pat dry thoroughly.

Heat the olive oil in a large saucepan. Add the onion and garlic and sauté until the onion is cooked. Add the undrained tomatoes, tomato paste, basil and oregano and bring the sauce to a boil. Simmer for about 30 minutes, or until well thickened. Season with salt and pepper.

In a large frying pan, heat the extra olive oil. Working in batches, fry the eggplant slices on both sides until cooked through and lightly golden. Add more oil as necessary. Drain the eggplant slices on paper towels.

Preheat the oven to 350°F (180°C/Gas 4).

Cook the pasta in boiling salted water until *al dente*. Drain and stir into the tomato sauce. Grease a large (8 cup [4 pint/2 l] capacity) gratin dish. Arrange the ingredients in the dish in the following sequence: one-third eggplant slices, half tomato pasta sauce, one-third eggplant slices, half mozzarella slices, half tomato pasta sauce, one-third eggplant slices, half mozzarella slices.

Bake, uncovered, for 30 minutes, or until the cheese on top is melted and golden.

Serves 6
Preparation/Cooking Time: 1 hour 30 minutes

Individual Ratatouille Lasagne

⅓ cup (3 fl oz/90 ml) olive oil
1 onion, diced
1 clove garlic, crushed
1 (14 oz/440 g) can peeled
    tomatoes, undrained
1 teaspoon tomato paste
salt and pepper
2 small–medium eggplants
    (aubergines)
1½ red bell peppers (capsicums)
4 zucchini (courgettes), topped,
    tailed, and blanched in boiling
    water

Béchamel Sauce:
1 tablespoon (½ oz/15 g) butter
2 tablespoons all-purpose (plain)
    flour
1 cup (8 fl oz/250 ml) milk
½ cup (4 fl oz/125 ml) heavy
    (whipping) cream

1 lb (500 g) lasagne noodles
1⅓ cups (5 oz/155 g) freshly
    grated Parmesan cheese
4 bocconcini mozzarella cheeses,
    sliced

Heat 2 tablespoons of the olive oil in a saucepan. Sauté the onion and garlic until soft. Add the canned tomatoes, tomato paste, and salt and pepper to taste. Simmer until reduced and thick. Set aside.

Slice the eggplants (aubergines) into rounds. Sprinkle the slices with salt and set aside for 30 minutes. Rinse and pat dry on paper towels. Heat the remaining oil in a skillet and fry the eggplant until golden on both sides. Set aside.

Halve the bell peppers (capsicums) and remove the seeds and membranes. Place the halves under a hot broiler (grill) and cook until their skin is blackened and blistered. Remove from broiler and place in a paper bag and seal. Set aside until cool. When cool remove the skin and cut the bell peppers into thick strips.

Béchamel Sauce: Melt the butter in a saucepan, stir in the flour and cook over low heat for 2 minutes. Off the heat, gradually stir in the milk and cream. Return to the heat and cook, stirring, until mixture thickens. Add salt to taste. Thin with a little extra milk, if necessary. Set aside.

Cook the lasagne according to the instructions on the packet. Drain and place on a flat surface in one layer until required.

Preheat the oven to 325°F (170°C/Gas 3).

Place 4 strips of lasagne in a lightly oiled baking dish. Spread each strip with a tablespoon of sauce. Top with tomato mixture and sprinkle on some Parmesan. Continue layers as follows: pasta, béchamel, zucchini, red bell pepper, Parmesan, pasta, béchamel sauce, eggplant, bocconcini slices, pasta. Spread top layer of pasta with béchamel sauce and sprinkle with Parmesan. Place baking dish in the preheated oven and heat until warmed through and the bocconcini has melted, 30–40 minutes.

Serves 4
Preparation/Cooking Time: 1 hour

Asparagus and Ham Lasagne Rolls

1 sheet (about 1 lb/500 g) fresh
   pasta, cut into 8 equal squares
13 oz (400 g) fresh asparagus
1 cup (3½ oz/100 g) freshly
   grated Parmesan cheese
13 oz (400 g/8 slices) boiled ham

Béchamel Sauce:
7 tablespoons (3½ oz/100 g)
   butter
3 tablespoons all-purpose (plain)
   flour
1½ cups (12 fl oz/375 ml) milk
½ cup (4 fl oz/125 ml) dry white
   wine
½ cup (4 fl oz/125 ml) light
   (single) cream

Bring a large quantity of water to a boil in a large pot. Drop in the pasta squares, one or two at a time, and cook for 2–3 minutes, or until they are just *al dente*. Remove the pasta squares from the water and drain on clean tea towels.

Cook the asparagus in boiling water until just tender. Drain and run under cold water.

Béchamel Sauce: Melt the butter in a saucepan, add the flour and stir to form a roux. Cook gently for 1–2 minutes. Remove the saucepan from the heat. Gradually stir in the milk, then the wine. Return the saucepan to the heat and cook, stirring constantly, until the mixture boils and thickens. Stir in the cream and warm through, without boiling. Cover and set aside until required.

Preheat the oven to 350°F (180°C/Gas 4).

Lay out the pasta squares and spread 1 tablespoon of béchamel sauce over each. Sprinkle each with 1 tablespoon grated Parmesan. Top each sheet with 1 slice of ham and 3–4 spears of asparagus. Roll up the sheets and secure with a toothpick, if necessary. Place the rolls side by side in a greased ceramic baking dish. Pour on the remaining béchamel sauce, ensuring that each roll is well coated. Sprinkle with the remaining Parmesan.

Bake uncovered, for about 30 minutes, or until the top is golden and bubbling.

Serves 4. This makes an excellent luncheon dish served with a green salad.
Preparation/Cooking Time: 1 hour

Red Bell Peppers Stuffed with Orzo and Tuna

4 tablespoons olive oil

1 onion, finely chopped

2 cloves garlic, crushed

1 (14 oz/440 g) can tomatoes, undrained

1 tablespoon tomato paste

1 tablespoon chopped fresh basil

1 tablespoon chopped fresh oregano

1 tablespoon chopped parsley

4 oz (125 g) orzo (risoni) — small pasta, similar to rice

1 (6 oz/185 g) can tuna, preferably Italian style, drained and flaked

2 teaspoons tiny capers

8 black olives, pitted and chopped

2 large well-shaped red bell peppers (capsicums)

6½ oz (200 g) mozzarella cheese, sliced

1 (2 oz/60 g) can flat anchovy fillets

1 cup (3½ oz/100 g) freshly grated Parmesan cheese

freshly ground black pepper

Heat two tablespoons of the oil in saucepan and gently sauté the onion and garlic until the onion is cooked. Stir in the tomatoes, tomato paste, and herbs. Simmer, uncovered, for 25 minutes, until the sauce is well thickened. Remove from heat.

Cook the orzo (risoni) in boiling salted water until *al dente*. Drain thoroughly.

Add the tuna, capers, olives, and orzo (risoni) to the sauce. Stir thoroughly. Preheat oven to 350°F (180°C/Gas 4).

Cut the bell peppers (capsicums) in half lengthwise, and remove all seeds and membrane. Spoon the filling into the peppers and smooth the surface. Arrange the bell peppers snugly in a baking dish and spoon over the remaining 2 tablespoons oil. Bake the bell peppers for 40 minutes.

Remove from the oven, top with the mozzarella, and then the anchovies in criss-cross pattern. Sprinkle on the grated Parmesan, pepper to taste and a little more oil. Return the peppers to the oven and bake for 10 minutes, or until the cheese is golden. Serve immediately.

Serves 4
Preparation/Cooking Time: 1 hour 30 minutes

Stuffed Pasta Shells in Tomato Sauce

3 tablespoons olive oil
2 onions, chopped
2 cloves garlic, chopped
1 (14 oz/440 g) can plum
  tomatoes, undrained
2–3 bay leaves
1 tablespoon tomato paste
24 giant pasta shells

Filling:
3 cups (1½ lb/750 g) ricotta cheese
1 cup (1 oz/30 g) shredded basil
1 egg, beaten
5 oz (155 g) spicy salami, sliced
  and cut into julienne
salt and black pepper

White Wine Sauce:
2 tablespoons butter
2 tablespoons all-purpose (plain)
  flour
1 cup (8 fl oz/250 ml) milk
½ cup (4 fl oz/125 ml) dry white
  wine

6½ oz (200 g) mozzarella cheese
½ cup (1¾ oz/50 g) freshly grated
  Parmesan cheese

Heat the oil in a large saucepan. Add the onions and garlic and cook until the onion is soft. Add the tomatoes, bay leaves and tomato paste. Bring to a boil, then simmer over low heat for 20–30 minutes, until sauce is reduced and thick.

Cook pasta in boiling salted water until *al dente*. Drain.

Filling: Combine all the ingredients in a bowl and mix thoroughly. Fill the pasta shells using a teaspoon.

Preheat the oven to 350°F (180°C/Gas 4).

White Wine Sauce: Melt the butter in a saucepan, add the flour and stir to form a roux. Cook very gently for 1–2 minutes. Remove the saucepan from the heat. Gradually stir in the milk then the wine. Return the saucepan to the heat and cook, stirring constantly, until the mixture boils and thickens. Reduce the heat and cook gently for 1–2 minutes.

Remove the bay leaves from the tomato sauce. Pour the sauce into an 8-cup capacity, shallow, ovenproof dish. Arrange the stuffed pasta shells in the middle of the dish. Pour on half the white wine sauce. Top the pasta shells with thinly-sliced mozzarella and pour on the remaining white wine sauce. Finally, sprinkle with grated Parmesan.

Bake for 20–25 minutes, or until the top is golden. Finish under the broiler (grill), if necessary.

Serves 6–8
Preparation/Cooking Time: 1 hour

84

Cannelloni Stuffed with Ham and Ricotta

Sauce:

2 tablespoons olive oil

1 large onion, finely chopped

2 cloves garlic, crushed

*1 (28 oz/880 g) can peeled plum
    tomatoes, undrained*

1½ tablespoons tomato paste

*2 tablespoons chopped fresh basil
    leaves*

*salt and freshly ground black
    pepper*

1 lb (500 g) cannelloni tubes

1 cup (8 oz/250 g) ricotta cheese

2 thick slices cooked ham, diced

1 egg

*salt and freshly ground black
    pepper*

*3½ oz (100 g) freshly grated
    Parmesan cheese*

Sauce: Heat the oil and sauté the onion and garlic until the onion is soft. Add the tomatoes and their juice, the tomato paste, basil, salt and pepper. Bring the sauce to a boil, reduce the heat and simmer for 30 minutes, or until the sauce is smooth and thick.

While the sauce is cooking, prepare the cannelloni. If the cannelloni tubes are not precooked, boil them in boiling salted water until they are *al dente*.

Preheat the oven to 350°F (180°C/Gas 4).

In a bowl, combine all the ricotta, ham, egg and salt and pepper until thoroughly blended.

Using a teaspoon, carefully stuff the filling generously into the tubes. Arrange the filled tubes in a single layer in a well greased, shallow baking dish. Pour over the sauce and ensure that all the tubes are covered. Sprinkle on the grated Parmesan. Bake for 30 minutes, or until the top is nicely browned.

Serves 4
Preparation/Cooking Time: 1 hour

Lemon Pasta Envelopes with Cream Cheese Filling

Pasta:

2⅔ cups (10 oz/315 g) all-
purpose (plain) flour
1 tablespoon superfine (caster)
sugar
grated zest of 2 lemons
juice of 1 large lemon
1 egg, beaten

Filling:

⅔ cup (5 oz/155 g) ricotta cheese
6½ oz (200 g) cream cheese
2 teaspoons grated lemon zest
1 tablespoon lemon juice
½ cup (3½ oz/100 g) superfine
(caster) sugar
2 eggs, separated
⅓ cup (1¾ oz/50 g) golden
raisins (sultanas)

1 beaten egg, for sealing
vegetable oil, for deep-frying
confectioners' (icing) sugar
fresh berries of your choice

Place the dry pasta ingredients and lemon zest in a food processor. Process briefly. Add the lemon juice and egg and process until the mixture forms a ball. Add a little more lemon juice, if necessary. Cover and let the pasta dough rest for 15 minutes.

Filling: Beat the ricotta and cream cheese with an electric mixer or food processor, until smooth. Beat in the lemon zest, lemon juice and superfine (caster) sugar. Beat in the egg yolks, one at a time. Fold in the raisins (sultanas). Beat the egg whites in a bowl until soft peaks form. Fold into the cheese mixture.

Divide the pasta into four parts. Roll out each piece into a very thin sheet. Using a pasta cutter, cut the pasta into 4-inch (10-cm) squares. Working a few at a time, paint around the edges of each square with a little beaten egg. Place a tablespoon of the filling in the center of each square, then fold it like an envelope to completely enclose the filling. (The envelopes can be sealed with a pasta shape of your choice, e.g. heart, if desired. Brush the back of the shape with beaten egg before applying.)

Heat sufficient oil in a saucepan to deep-fry the envelopes. Deep-fry them, one at a time, for about 30 seconds, until golden. Drain on paper towels. When the envelopes are sufficiently cool, dust with confectioners' (icing) sugar.

Serve warm or at room temperature, with fresh berries of your choice.

Serves 4
Preparation/Cooking Time: 1 hour

Fresh Figs with Almond Mascarpone and Deep-fried Pasta Wedges

*4 strips dry lasagne — not
  precooked*
Vegetable oil for deep-frying
1 egg white
*⅔ cup (2½ oz/75 g) slivered
  (flaked) almonds, lightly toasted*
Confectioners' (icing) sugar
1 cup (7 oz/220 g) sugar
1 cup (8 fl oz/250 ml) hot water
1 tablespoon red wine
4 fresh figs —1 per person
2 tablespoons Kirsch
4 oz (125 g) almond macaroons
8 oz (250 g) mascarpone cheese

Cook the lasagne strips in boiling salted water until *al dente*. Drain and dry on clean tea towels. Cut the lasagne into any desired shape and size.

Preheat the oven to 350°F (180°C/Gas 4).

Heat sufficient oil to deep-fry the lasagne pieces. Deep-fry the pasta, one piece at a time, until golden. Remove from the oil, place on paper towels and allow to cool. Brush the fried pasta pieces with a little egg white and press on the almonds. Place on a baking sheet and bake for 5 minutes. Remove from oven and cool. Dust with confectioners' (icing) sugar.

To make the sugar glaze: Combine the granulated sugar, water and wine in a saucepan. Bring to a boil and continue boiling until the sugar dissolves and the mixture thickens to a syrup consistency. Allow to cool.

Quarter the figs and arrange on individual serving dishes. Sprinkle with the Kirsch and brush with the sugar syrup.

Place the macaroons in a food processor and process to form a crumb mixture. In a bowl, mix the crumbs with the mascarpone. Moisten with extra Kirsch, if necessary. Spoon some mascarpone mixture onto each serving dish and add two deep-fried pasta wedges. The remainder of the wedges can be served in a bowl for passing around the table.

Serves 4
Preparation/Cooking Time: 45 minutes

Individual Orzo Puddings

½ cup (2½ oz/75 g) orzo (risoni)

½ cup (4 fl oz/125 ml) heavy
(whipping) cream

1½ cups (12 fl oz/375 ml) milk

⅓ cup (2½ oz/75 g) superfine
(caster) sugar

2 teaspoons vanilla extract
(essence)

2 teaspoons finely grated orange
zest

2 whole eggs

1 egg yolk

1 tablespoon orange marmalade

1 tablespoons Grand Marnier
liqueur

Cook the orzo (risoni) in boiling salted water until *al dente*. Drain and set aside.

Preheat the oven to 350°F (180°C/Gas 4).

Combine the cream, milk, sugar, vanilla and orange zest in a saucepan. Stir over low heat, without boiling, until the sugar is dissolved. Add the orzo, bring to a boil, and simmer for 3 minutes. Remove from the heat.

Beat the eggs and egg yolk in a bowl. Gradually beat them into the milk mixture. Divide the resulting custard among six ½ cup (4 fl oz/125 ml) ramekins. Place the ramekins in a large baking dish. Add enough boiling water to come halfway up the sides of the ramekins. Bake for 1 hour.

Combine the marmalade and Grand Marnier in a small saucepan and warm gently.

Remove the ramekins from the baking dish and brush the tops with the combined jam and liqueur. Serve the puddings warm.

Serves 6
Preparation/Cooking Time: 1 hour 30 minutes